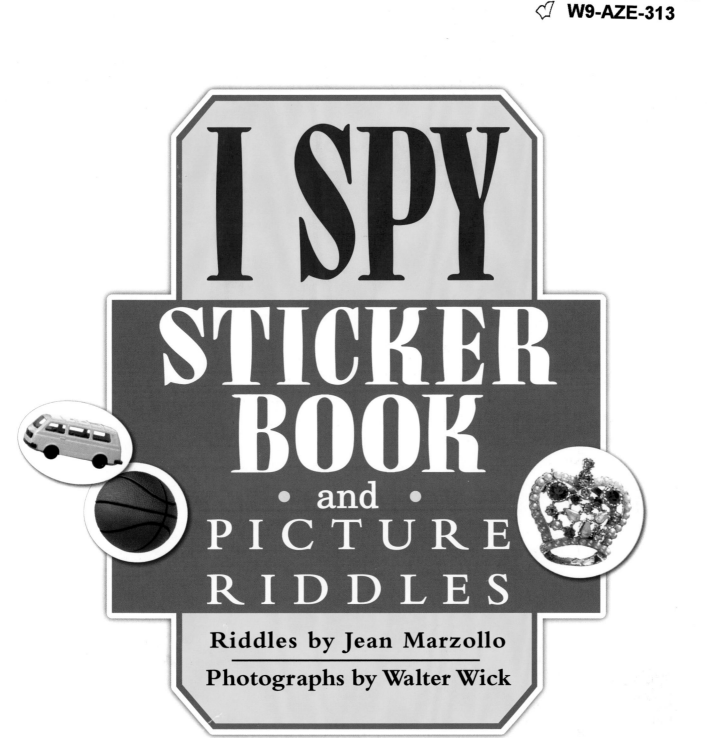

# I SPY
# STICKER
# BOOK
## · and ·
# PICTURE
# RIDDLES

### Riddles by Jean Marzollo
### Photographs by Walter Wick

Scholastic Inc.
New York  Toronto  London  Auckland
Sydney  Mexico City  New Delhi  Hong Kong

a caboose,

 a dinosaur's eye,

a large yellow e,

and a plane that can fly.

I spy

a bike,

 a car with a 9,

a ball with an 8,

 and a milk
truck sign.

a fish,

a sparkly bow tie,

a blue guitar,

and a butterfly.

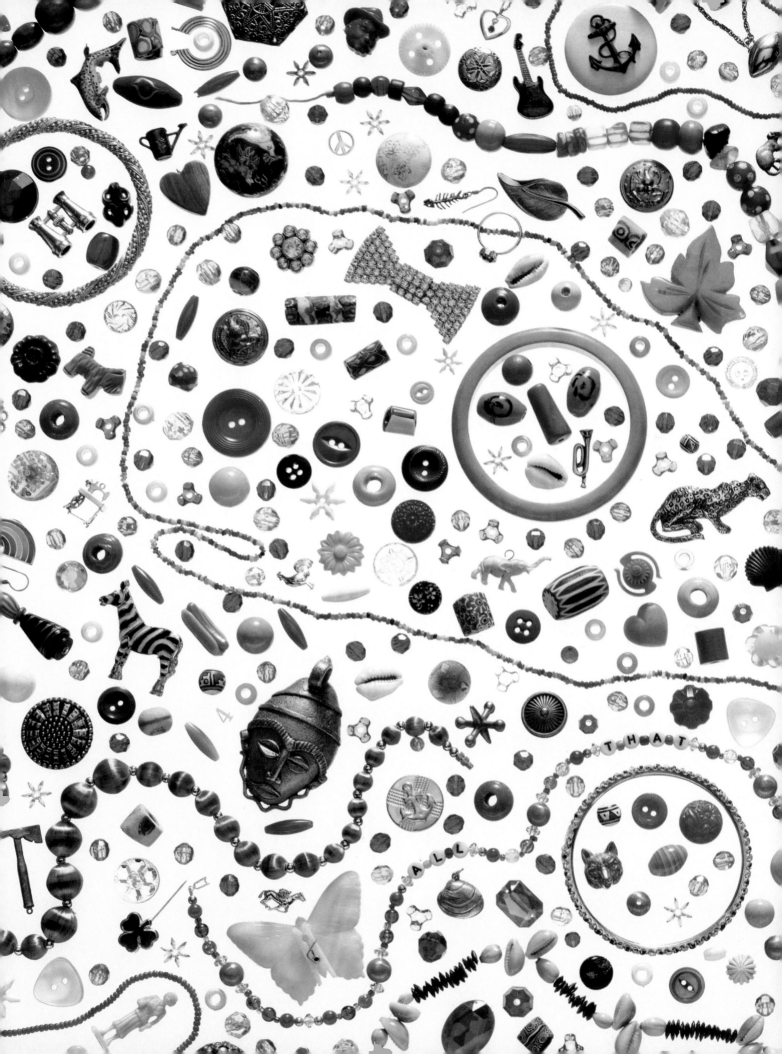

 I spy

a brush,

 a dancer on toes,

a black spider,

 and a bunny
in clothes.

I spy

a ladder,

 a kangaroo,

a little heart,

 and a blue kazoo.

I spy

a flamingo,

a red bull's-eye,

a yellow umbrella,

and a blue bow tie.

a shovel,

a metal key,

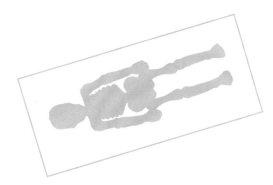 a skeleton,

and a golfer's tee.

I spy

a starfish,

 a happy seal,

a magnifying glass,

 and a silver
ship's wheel.

I spy

an eggbeater,

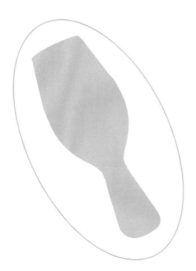

a blue bowling pin,

a yellow fire hydrant,

and an orange tail fin.

 I spy

 red lips,

a small metal ax,

 a turtle that glows,

and two silver jacks.

I spy

an angel,

 an egg split in two,

a two-headed dragon,

and a hat that is blue.

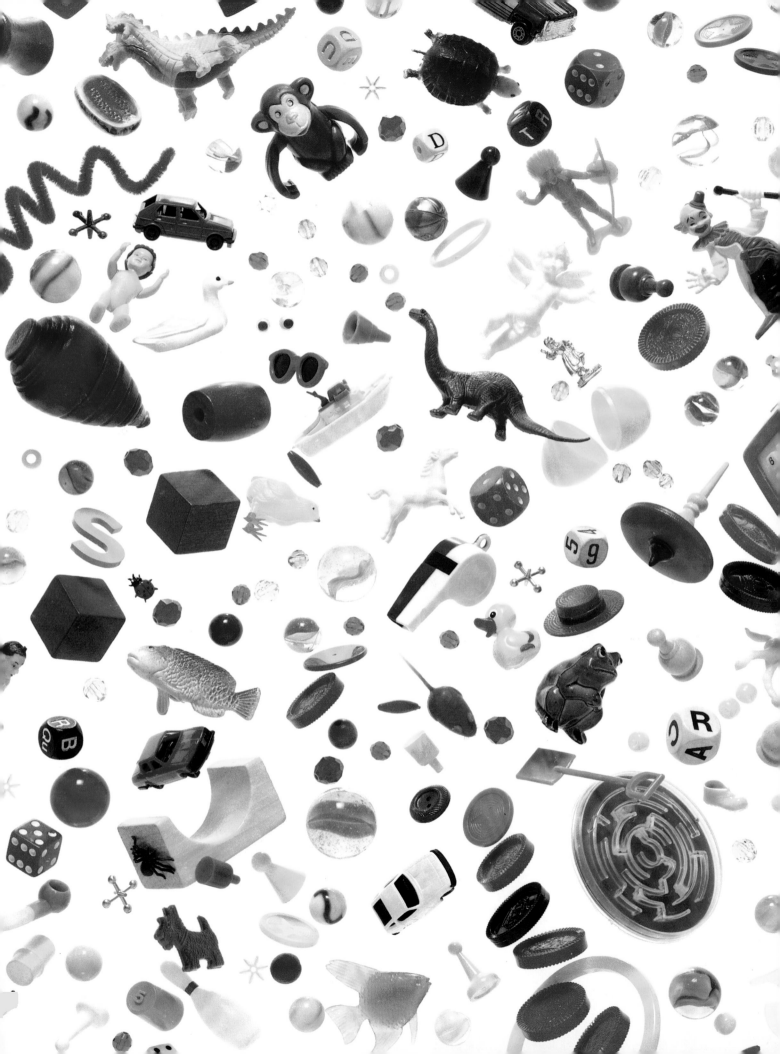

a soccer ball,

 a buzzing bee,

a little dog,

 and a pot of tea.

I spy

a green star,

 an apron that's white,

a little dump truck,

and a red flashlight.

I spy

a horse,

 a red-and-white ball,

a musical note,

and a train that's small.

a cowboy hat,

 a red cart,

a green dinosaur,

 and a block with a heart.

an anteater,

 a tasty hot dog,

a silver lock,

 and a spotted frog.

# I SPY PEOPLE

Made by _____

I spy a clown and a crown.
What else do I spy?

# I SPY SPORTS AND GAMES

Made by _____

I spy a tee and a left-foot ski.
What else do I spy?

# I SPY ANIMALS

Made by _____

I spy a dog and a frog.
What else do I spy?

# I SPY ANIMALS

Made by _____

I spy a bat and a cat.
What else do I spy?

# I SPY VEHICLES

## Made by _____

I spy a train and a plane.
What else do I spy?

# I SPY FOOD

Made by _____

I spy cheese and ice cream, please.
What else do I spy?

# I SPY ANYTHING GOES

Made by _____

## What do I spy?
## What do you spy?

# RIDDLE STICKERS

spider

musical note

shovel

turtle

train

blue bow tie

car

dinosaur

kazoo

hot dog

jacks

butterfly

soccer ball

red bull's-eye

eggbeater

flashlight

# RIDDLE STICKERS

dancer

dragon

frog

fish

ship's wheel

caboose

key

flamingo

fire hydrant

baseball

plane

cart

block with
a heart

guitar

starfish

# RIDDLE STICKERS

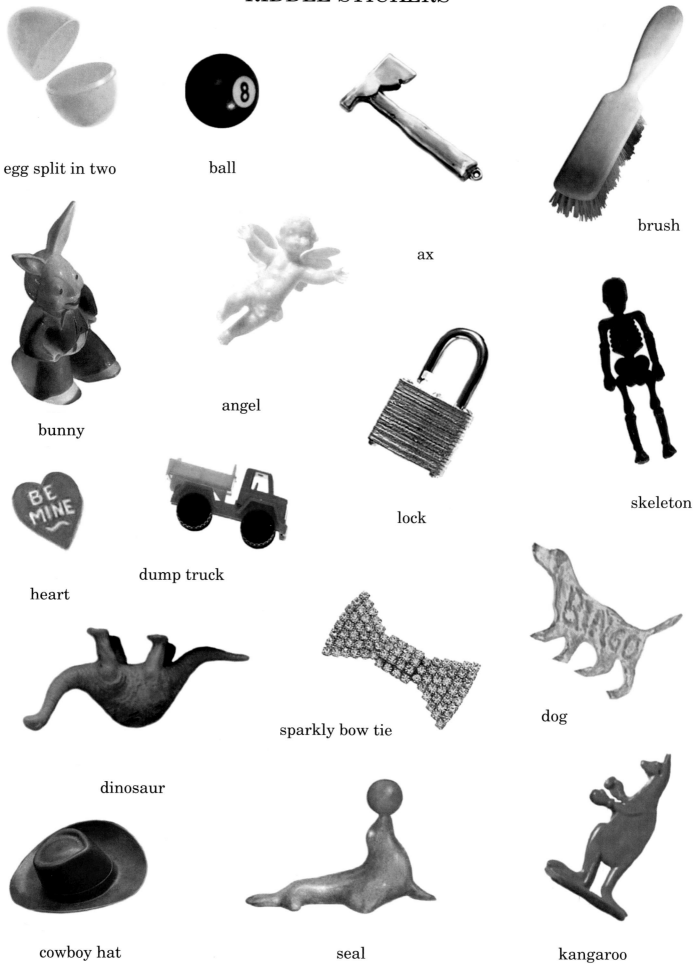

egg split in two

ball

ax

brush

bunny

angel

lock

skeleton

heart

dump truck

sparkly bow tie

dog

dinosaur

cowboy hat

seal

kangaroo

# RIDDLE STICKERS

large yellow e

teapot

lips

bike

ladder

white apron

golfer's tee

hat

bee

anteater

magnifying glass

star

umbrella

bowling pin

milk truck

fish

horse

# "MAKE YOUR OWN" STICKERS

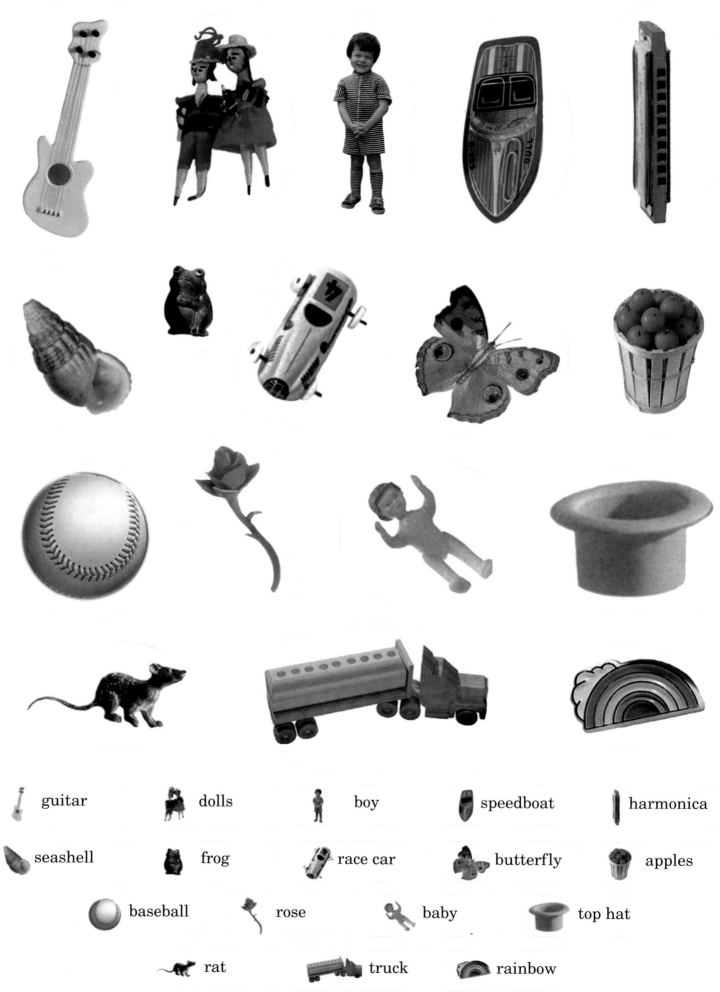

guitar · dolls · boy · speedboat · harmonica

seashell · frog · race car · butterfly · apples

baseball · rose · baby · top hat

rat · truck · rainbow

# "MAKE YOUR OWN" STICKERS

# "MAKE YOUR OWN" STICKERS

teeth     car     guitar     valentine     cat

duck     ball     roller skate     fisherman     wolf

dolphin     boat     horn

cyclist     doll     puppy

apple     pipe     skateboard     golf ball

# "MAKE YOUR OWN" STICKERS

# "MAKE YOUR OWN" STICKERS

# "MAKE YOUR OWN" STICKERS

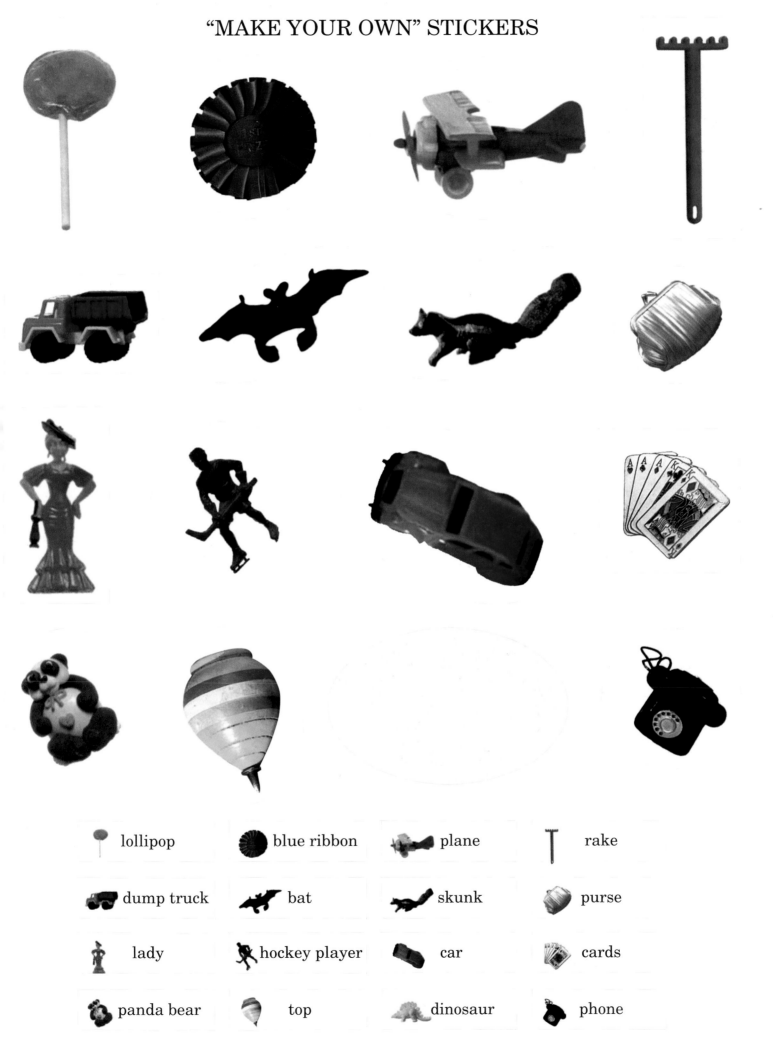

| | | | |
|---|---|---|---|
| lollipop | blue ribbon | plane | rake |
| dump truck | bat | skunk | purse |
| lady | hockey player | car | cards |
| panda bear | top | dinosaur | phone |

# "MAKE YOUR OWN" STICKERS

ball    compass    lion    badge

surfer    saxophone    basketball player    pliers    pirate

face    tiger    helicopter    firefighter

motorcycle    dog    cement truck    boxing glove    pie

# "MAKE YOUR OWN" STICKERS

| | | | | |
|---|---|---|---|---|
| crab | cowboy boot | bell | man | yo-yo |
| woman | snowflake | fish | spinner | globe |
| fire truck | boat | football | truck | |
| broom | astronaut | key | plane | stingray |
| peas | car | | | |

# "MAKE YOUR OWN" STICKERS

| | | | |
|---|---|---|---|
| lizard | ice-cream cone | sea horse | scissors |
| French fries | strong man | skater | house of cards |
| puzzle piece | car | magnet | drumstick | ring |
| horn | drum | car | elephant | pinecone |

# "MAKE YOUR OWN" STICKERS

baseball player    fish    drum    accordion

lamb    nest    zebra    groom    peanuts

shovel    die    seagull

knight    robot    sailboat    police car    harp

train    sword

# MINI-STICKERS

# MINI-STICKERS